Skeletons in the Closet

This book will have sensitive content to some readers

This book will talk about, but not excluded to

Suicide   depression   death
         paranoia schizophrenia self-harm   nonconsenting sex   self-hatred   mental illnesses
        graphic imaging   abuse

Please read with care
        this book is meant to be a voice   not a weapon

Thank you and take care love

-N

Readers discretion is advised

Thank you to the princess turned Queen who guided me home. To the Guide who helped me get back on my feet and to my loving friends and family who support me. Thank you for wanting to hear my voice.

I:
The Body Bags

Cookies

she slipped her hands
around my throat
words catching on my lips
her poison seeped into my skin
flowing through my body
three fingers slit my throat
and I laid in a pool of my own self worth
while she smiled and baked cookies

never again

Signs

    I was looking

                    for the signs

        the ones with

                          skulls and bones

    I didn't think   you
                        were hiding them

behind

            my

                        back

Security Blanket

he wrapped me up in a blanket
full of love and desire
only later will I find out
that it was made of barbed wire

Bones I

there's a soft vibration I feel
the pulse crawls through my skin
my limbs ache and moan
and my body catches heat
you've contaminated my bones

now they're burning

like the coals of a late summer

nights fire

Bones II

I've thrown out my clothes
    pulled out my hair
        peeled back my skin
            and burned my clothes
            and yet my skeleton
                still itches to the thought
                of you

Bones III

we've danced under the night sky twice

the first time – the clock had stuck twelve

I ran away back home

something was missing

I didn't walk the same

until we danced again

this time you ran away when the clock chimed twelve

and behind you

you left one of my bones

you no longer owned a piece of me

Gone?

why is it that the dead

stay longer than

the living

Faceless Names

Alone and dark

skeptical and skittish. Frightened shadows and hollowed minds. Autopilots and kamikazes, hijackers and rookies. Swallowed by grief swallowed by pride. Swallowed by hollowed mindless puppets. Shattered by dreams built by reality. Old news brings new pain. Latest news brings suffering. The dead still live but the living doesn't exist. Unnamed faces cover those named. Family air looms are nothing but graves. Any stick can be a weapon. Any person can be a killer. Anybody can try to justify. Anybody can roll over and die. Everyone can die.

Even the hollowed puppets attached to bigger hands

This will kill me one day

I Wonder

sometimes I wonder
what my life would be like
if I had stayed in therapy
if I had taken the shots
the pills
if had changed my name
gotten the surgeries
sometimes I wonder
how life would be
but then I think of my family
they're supporting no doubt
but they aren't ready for a change
and maybe I'm not either
I don't regret stopping the therapy
what I do regret
is having my mother plaster a fake smile

as the child she's only known for such a short while

suddenly isn't there anymore

I regret making my mother cry

I regret making my brother confused more than he already is

and I regret leaving my dad in the dark

I was gone for so long

and then when I came back

I was changing everything

I'm sorry

Thorns

pretty versus flowed from their fingers
enchanting phrases

fulfilling promises

they swept you off your feet
and bathed you in flowers

when you accepted their promise
all you felt were thorns

Flawed I

Humans are empty

they constantly look for something to fill a void

they are always looking for a plan or routine

cars dating TV

kids work music art

school sex drugs

gambling alcohol

Humans are flawed

they are flawed because they are unfinished products of evolution

Humans are flawed

because they are aware

that they aren't complete

Flawed II

I'm scared to look in that void

I'm aware it's not empty

there is something inside of me I don't want to meet

it will try to devour me

which one of us is really in the dark

Flawed III

they're toxic to your mental health

if you must question

their morals

Drag

It was just curiosity

        just a taste

An opportunity I didn't want to waste

I pulled in the first drag

    the smoke filling my lungs

it was supposed to hurt

        but it was like a hug

the smoke left my lips

it curled down around my hips

the crisp midnight air

showed the cloud of smoke

        I just stare

it was just a taste on my tongue

I didn't think it would last long

I was a thief who was stuck

of course I'd run out of luck

    I was caught red handed

      didn't know this is where it would land me

it's been five years now
I don't know how
a cloud of smoke formed a hand
and put my feet back on land

Every day

I lost my voice

not once or twice

every day my words catch fire

the smoke will fill my lungs

black smog will stain my tongue

my words will turn to ash

and my train of thought will crash

every day I lose my voice

mouth sewn shut

all my words are washed away

by the glare you give me

every day

Pawn I

Pawn to E4

I was young and naïve

I believed there was good in everyone

I believed there was good in you

when you came to me

a stranger none the less

you begged for an ear

I gave you my whole soul

I listened to each of your tales

tears streamed down my face

I sympathized with you

I fell victim to your games

you played me right into your hand

there- I stayed for awhile

I was your pawn

Pawn to D5

Pawn II

Pawn to D5

the original voice that burrowed in my head

was supposedly long gone

a new face had taken their place

hours were spent talking to each other

phone calls and video chats

on opposites sides of the world

a romance was blossoming

its roots twisting together

we went through changes together

I had completely forgotten

that there was still a little voice

that had burrowed inside my head

Bishop to G4

Pawn III

Pawn to D6

I thought I had known who you were

I had seen your face   had heard your voice

one day you made a confession

you weren't who you played to be

you weren't the voice I had known for two years

you were the voice I sought out to help

the voice that betrayed me and left in the night

you claimed to have wanted to get to know me

to be my friend   to be apart of my life

so you played this game to get me to open up

well I will end this

Bishop to D1

The queen is down

The Inner Voice

Sex is good

> *You're a slut*

Sex is bad

> *You're a prude*

I was raped

> *No, you weren't*

I raped him

> *Men can't be raped*

I didn't want to

> *You didn't say no*

I wanted to

> *You're a dirty whore*

Sex scares me

> *You're missing out*

I love sex

> *Close your legs for once*

I'm waiting till marriage

> *You're a hussy*

I was introduced to sex at an early age

    You're a needy cunt

I didn't enjoy it

    *But you were **wet***

I didn't want to

    *But you said **yes***

I was pressured into sex

    You wanted it

He wouldn't leave me alone

    *You wanted **it***

He just kept whining and asking me to do it

    *You **wanted it***

It was our first time meeting

    You wanted it

Because you're a girl

Women were made for men

I didn't want this

II:

The Autopsy

Lines

they don't want to die

                    they just want to be alive

Ijustneededtofeelalive

Light

we take light for granted

we don't think of light as useful

until we are shrouded in darkness

then all we do is pray for a light

that has abandoned us

I Live in a Box Now

when a light goes out in my house

I'll try to burn down the house

Sometimes

sometimes I cry
        for no reason
sometimes I'm angry
        for no reason
sometimes I'm anxious
        for no reason
sometimes I'm sexual
        for no reason
sometimes I want to die
        for no reason

is this normal?

I can only win

This fight

If I take these pills

Risks

when I risk the chance

or making someone late

or hurting someone

or making someone upset

I will unintentionally hurt myself

risk my own life

or

do nothing

I'm sorry for scaring you

and almost crashing into that other car

trying to get you to work

Religion

I'm not religious

but I grew up religious

I went to church every Sunday with my friends

only because Saturday was the only day for sleepovers, I had to go

when I was six I didn't understand

when I was seven I didn't understand

when I turned ten she abandoned me in His name

when I was eleven these siblings told me their dad would hit me because I used His name in vain

when I was twelve I visit a youth group

I felt unclean in the church

I didn't belong

when I was fifteen he swore by God and left when he discovered who I was

I visit a youth group and a church

I hear their words

I don't belong with them

because I'm not religious

I feel like a sheep in lions clothing

I am not who people want me to be

I Don't Blame You

at the time you were my best friend

the first friend I made

it was a new town

fresh faces

a new home

you had brought me into your life

yet you treated me like a child

I was young   yes

but so were you

you followed the way of God

you made me fear him

you tried to make me follow that path but I couldn't

then one day I hit a bump in my road

I had started going down a dark path

but I didn't realize it at the time

my friends said it was a cool thing to do

so I did it with them

not knowing why

when I turned to you, excited to what I had done to my own body

you turned me away

you were ready to terminate our friendship

so I lied

but you saw through that

a year later we grew apart

and now

sometimes I forget you live next door

that you have for ten years

sometimes I forget that at one point

you were like my sister

I guess God had other plans for you

please take care.

Viper and the King

he convinced you
        that you were the villain
he was the victim
        crying every night because you did
            nothing
        that what you did was wrong
he twisted his words
        to form a noose around your heart
he stabbed you in the back
    but your fingerprints were on the knife
he made a safety net out of lies
he'd catch you when you fell
        but you were on solid ground
            with no way of falling
he dug a hole for your demise
        and pushed you in

VicToMisery

    it's not what I don't know that I fear

    but the known threats that can lie in a friend

    or become the outcome of a beautiful thing

    victory turned misery

Why

I watched you two grow close

I was there the day she told you how she felt

I knew from the start you weren't the one for her

I think you both knew this

and yet you didn't stop and get off the train

you both were on

Sticks and Stones

you threw my heart into a cage

poked it with a stick

then dared to question why there was blood

Early Confusion

I was always mistaken for a boy

well now I'm confused as well

Salt

Ring around the Rosie's a game we play

we tag each other night and day

it's a never-ending circle

I don't even know if it'll work or

if this is how it's going to be

we're going to tag each other until one leaves

but maybe it's just all fun and games until

one of us loses the will

but I see myself getting better

even with each letter

I want to be a new person

I don't want my mindset to worsen

so I'll put in the effort to be this way

even if it only lasts for a day

I want to know if you'll do the same

or if none of this is worth a damn

Look Deeper

I look like a strong forest

but there's a fire with no smoke

    I look like a calm mountain

but lava is coursing through me

    I look like a stilled cliff

one rough move and I crumble

    I'm flowing green grass

but I die so easily

    I look like fluffy clouds

but I can rain down on you

    all you see is what you want to see

    not what's really going on

you don't look for signs of burning wood

you don't see the storm brewing behind you

shit happens

    even if you don't see it

Ashamed

I shouldn't have to feel ashamed

for calling people Daddy or Mommy

I shouldn't be ashamed that I'm living my childhood now

I was forced to grow up too soon

let me enjoy myself

Little Horrors I

I see things that aren't there

I hear voices whisper to me sometimes

I will have nightmares while I'm awake

and I will just lie in bed

watching behind my eyes

as the horror unfolds

I feel them

Little Horrors II

I can control my dreams

until I fall asleep

it's my favorite part of the day

but sometimes

my anxiety and paranoia come to visit

they creep up my body

digging their claws into me

and sit on my chest

my dreams will turn to nightmares

all I can do is sit and stare

it can't be stopped

        I can't move

        I can't breathe

        I can't open my eyes

        I'm crying but I can't wake up

        I know I'm dreaming

Little Horrors III

when I wake up

I move so sudden that it hurts

back against the wall as I stare into the dark pit of a room

the soft glow of a light illuminate's shadows on my wall

the dancing monsters that move across my bedroom floor

I coward into a corner

sobbing into nothing

a part of my body will be injured

most likely from myself

I will stare into my room and try to calm my racing heart

but then

I see its' eyes look up at me

Little Horrors IV

I haven't slept alone for eight years

there is something that watches me

I know there are more than one

I know they wait for me

I'm paranoid

III:

The Burial

Love

sometimes I think that humans use the term love

too loosely

love doesn't mean

I'm going to be by your side when you change your hair color

love doesn't mean

I want to have sex with you as much as possible

love doesn't mean

We have a lot in common

love doesn't mean

We'd be a cute couple

humans

doesn't matter gender or age

humans don't appreciate the feeling of love

don't confuse love for

Lust   Need   Romance   Longing   Fantasies   Attraction

these are not other words for love

don't ruin this feeling

Fed Up

it was a lust bound relationship
you argued every night
you both weren't happy
fed up with each other
I could hear it in the way she talked about you
I could see it in the way you held her
you both were fed up

Natural Disasters

                she was a

hurricane

                he was a

volcano

two natural disasters for their own world

the hurricane was used to sweeping up towns

flooding rivers and reshaping the land

the volcano was used to a world of fire

destroying life as it went its daily route

they left chaos in their trails

the only sign of life being themselves

self-destructive behavior

self-destructive minds

when two natural disasters meet

one will outlive the other

Toxic I

he was toxic

too toxic for me

his suicidal tendencies were too much for me

I was trying to recover

I knew I should've stayed

maybe I could have helped

but sometimes you need to watch your own war

before you fight someone else's

Toxic II

in her own way

she was toxic too

she was hurting inside

it was clear as day

she wore her heart on her sleeve

she dared anyone to point out that fact

intimidating to most

she was a ticking time bomb

ready to destroy herself at any moment

Toxic III

they fought every time I saw them

it could be about him   or about her

they both were hurting

one more than the other

two negatives drilled into each other

they made their despair worse

they wanted a family

he was young

they were engaged

it had been two months

a hospital trip   miscarriage

relapsing and tears

I knew from the start they weren't good for each other

    they built their love on lust

He Was Toxic

you didn't need to leave her

for someone else

you aren't stable

and neither is she

but you didn't need to leave her

for someone else

Addiction

I'm an addict

not to drugs

but to pain

addicted to self-hate   ruining my image

addicted to my own pleasure

addicted to hurting myself

in any way I could

I sabotage my relations   I betray myself

I'm an addict to being sad

to finding a reason   to destroy myself

I am a recovering addict

I found my way with faith

not religion

but faith that I will be different   that I will be okay

I am a recovering addict

because I met a princess who I hate seeing sad

I found a guide who loves me despite my past

I found myself

I won't be going back

9/15/17

we started at the same time

you took things more serious

at first it made me mad

like you were just copying me

but now I see

I gave you the courage

I opened your eyes a bit

now I couldn't be more proud

I'm sorry for being selfish

you helped me realize

that wasn't meant for me

thank you

One of these days

I will control

These thoughts

The Path

with everyone it's the same path

a change is something I lack

I never thought to change the way I thought

but the way I am is a hopeless battle I fought

I want to change the way I act

I want to make a pact-

with myself I want to be on track

I want to help myself and that's a fact

I don't know how to do it on my own

granted it makes me feel like a drone-

following your words everywhere I go

but it helps me not feel so low

right now you're just being yourself

I don't think you understand how much you help

to me you're like the stars guiding me to a home I never knew

you make me feel like there's nothing I can't do

when my boat starts to get thrown by waves

you step in and save the day

you bring my boat back to the bay

you ease my mind with every word you say

it's incredible

although it's debatable

whether or not you make my mind stable

you've touched parts of me

that never knew what being touched mean

I know you want to keep distant

for some it's just an instinct

that should be something I respect

but I can't help but to be so direct

usually I'm scared to fall for someone

because of all the pain that'll be done

but right now I don't feel that way

like I just woke up a new person one day

I'm getting too mushy again

this wasn't the plan   but things happen

Photography

      the world is monochrome
        heavy blacks and greys
      and one day you showed me
         color
      now I see the world through
colored   glasses

High Thoughts of You

I just want to hold your hand
memorize the way your fingers fit
how hard you grasp how warm you are
I want to feel the shivers up my arm
like electric bolts crawling on my skin
I want to feel your touch
nothing serious
just light brushes from your fingers
the way your skin sets fire to my own
I want to feel your heart
I'll match it with my own
I want to feel your vibe
get on the same level of life as you
I want to watch the sky
see the clouds turn to shapes
the stars falling
I want to hear your voice
how it calms me down

after a violent storm

I want to experience life with you

It's silly to say but I want to be with you

I want to say sorry for that

for the way you make me feel

I want to say sorry for everything

but I don't want to doubt this happiness

Zodiac Conspiracy

I don't know if these means anything
but all the important people in my life
are fish
all their birthdays are a day after each other
as a bull
this confuses me

Her Kingdom

she was a dream

she was the light breeze in the air

she was the leaves falling off summer trees

she was the clouds that wisp away into the sky

she was the river that crashed into the rocks

   she bent the world to her ways

she was the summer heat in July

  strong and overpowering

she was the first snow of winter

  delicate and beautiful

she washed everyone away with her words and stories

  a powerful tsunami in its peak

she could ruin a man by the sharp of her glare

she could bewitch any women with a turn of her lips

men admire from afar

  undeserving of her praise

women bowed to her

    caressing her in compliments

she was the match that lit the fire underneath trees

she was the drums that echoed through the mountains

she was as fierce as a Queen

    as fearless as a King

        she is her own army

        she is her own Kingdom

The Frog

there was a night

    not noble or bright

he rode in on his mule

    and confessed his love

blinded by his armor

the princess confessed her love as well

    for she could only see his shell

they traveled down the forest path

when something didn't feel quite right

he removed his helmet to whisper in her ear

his breath reeked of death and lust

without knowing   she had been bounded by rope

    attached to his hip

his words strangled the princess and suffocated her

the knight was a fraud

he begged her to stay; *a princess can be with a frog can't she?*

he trapped her free mind

he caged her spirit

took away her beauty and kept it as his own

the princess stood up for herself

    wrists bound by shackles

the frog of a knight wouldn't let her leave his sight

so one day she gathered all her might

turned into a dragon and took flight

now she watches guard of her own kingdom

while the frog sits and cowards in his pond

Funeral

I was digging my own grave
ready to slide in the coffin
when I saw her
standing there in all black
makeup stained cheeks
teary red eyes
I realized this was a funeral
but I wasn't ready to die

Home

it was dark and cold

numb to it all

I made my home

but I saw her again

tears smudged on her face

I wasn't ready to leave her

I packed my bags

I moved next door

she helped me make my new home

Bridges

we used to live

in the same town

but as the years grew on

we built our own towns

we may seem distant

but we built a bridge

from one to the other

I'm not going anywhere

IV:

The Eulogy

Painting

she was unaware of her own worth
like a priceless painting
unaware of how beautiful and timeless
she really was

Not You

I love him

I undeniably love him

he makes me feel like

I can build mountains

he makes me feel like I can take on the world

I love him

he pushes me to be a better person

he cheers me on and believes in me

he makes me feel powerful and strong

he believes in me

I loved him

he made me feel like I was snow on the sun

his hands felt like bolts of lightning on my thighs

I sighed every time his lips would touch mine

he loved me too

I loved him
I saw a future together
I saw a ring and a house
he understood my fears and made me better
I thought he saw it too

I lost him
he left with the door open
he left with my heart open
on his way out he broke everything I owned
on his way out he left holes in the wall
he left me without a word

I lost him
he left without leaving
he shattered me without using his hands
he threw me in the dark
but he left the door unlocked
he broke an already broken piece of art

I loathe him

he kept me in a cage

he made me think it was my idea

he was cold as ice and never loved me

I was an October fire looking for a forest to burn

I don't miss him

I miss the love I thought we had

I miss having someone's hands on me

I miss the lips on my neck

I miss a warm body next to mine

I don't miss him

I miss the laughs and jokes

I miss the planning of a future

I miss how full my heart had felt

I miss how good it felt

But I don't miss you

Frost Bite

I refused to be hurt anymore by the cold

the way it slowly takes you whole

how it started off with just a chilled nose

and then numbing in your toes

it sneaks up and takes your whole body

all you can think of is warmth

but all you get are icicles

I refuse to be frozen

I am not a body of water out in the woods

I am not a flower covered in snow

I am not the grass that dies from the blizzard

I am fire

I overpower the snow

I cannot and will not be frozen by you

I will melt my own path and drive you back to the mountain

I am a match thrown at trees

I am a blazing force that will not be stopped

I am a flame that will melt your blizzard

I am a flame that will never bow to the cold

I am my own warmth

I will not be frozen

I will win this fight

Paws

girls aren't easier

guys aren't any better

humans aren't perfect

some will take advantage

most will never give you a chance

but there is one person you can count on

they'll always be there for you

they'll love you when you can't even lift your head up in the morning

they don't care what you look like or what kind of person you are

they will never judge you

just always remember

to give them love and feed them

our pets are people too

they're just a bit different

but they love us the same

Too Good

you're too good for people
the type of people who don't care
you gave in to make them

stop

Consent

consent doesn't mean just "yes"

Them

if you can't do it for yourself

do it for them

Color

lines are only there

to show where you can color

not how you should color

make your own lines

Kindness

you fought other people's battles
just so they won't get hurt
yet when they see your wounds
they abandon you
you fought somebody else's war
and was exiled for kindness

Accept

you don't have to know

who you are

to accept yourself

Natures Beauty

roses are lovely

some people prefer lilies or tulips

maybe sunflowers and orchids

someone may prefer a plant to a daisy

then there are people who don't like flowers

perhaps someone might not know their favorite flower

maybe someone can't tell others what flower they like because its not what others like

or maybe

you're like me and love everything nature has to offer

Be You

you have the rest of your life
   to figure out
      who you are
         that might change
      a lot
         but it's okay
         don't stress
         just be you

Set in Stone

they say you can't tell

what gender you like

until you've tried them both

that's a load of bull

it's not about experience

although it may help

you don't need to have intercourse with multiple genders to see which one you like

it's more of a feeling

what feels right to you

and that may change

sexuality isn't set in stone

just like your personality isn't set in stone

who you are isn't who you'll always be

nothing is set in stone

feel free to rewrite your own story

or start writing it at your own pace

you are your own person

make sure you're happy

nobody else needs to be happy with your decisions

only you

With Love,

Gender identity

Sexuality

And

Gender

Are three different things

Please do not confuse them

-love, your friendly neighborhood queer

You

you'll be okay

that test isn't worth stressing over

that girl isn't worth the time of day

that guy isn't going to make things different

school is such a small part of your life

don't judge everything based off those few years

you don't have to go to college

you don't have to go to that university

you don't have to play that instrument

you don't have to dress like that for him to notice you

go get that tattoo

dye your hair crazy colors

shave your head

it's just hair

you can wear that if you want to

nobody cares what car you drive

the average human life span is 79-90 years

you aren't even half way there yet

some may not even be a fourth of the way there

you have your whole life

don't stress about it the whole time

don't worry my love

you'll be okay

I   Won

Made in the USA
Columbia, SC
13 December 2022